EXPLORING THE STATES

Louisiana

THE PELICAN STATE

by Lisa Owings

BLASTOFF! READERS
5

BELLWETHER MEDIA • MINNEAPOLIS, MN

Note to Librarians, Teachers, and Parents:

Blastoff! Readers are carefully developed by literacy experts and combine standards-based content with developmentally appropriate text.

Level 1 provides the most support through repetition of high-frequency words, light text, predictable sentence patterns, and strong visual support.

Level 2 offers early readers a bit more challenge through varied simple sentences, increased text load, and less repetition of high-frequency words.

Level 3 advances early-fluent readers toward fluency through increased text and concept load, less reliance on visuals, longer sentences, and more literary language.

Level 4 builds reading stamina by providing more text per page, increased use of punctuation, greater variation in sentence patterns, and increasingly challenging vocabulary.

Level 5 encourages children to move from "learning to read" to "reading to learn" by providing even more text, varied writing styles, and less familiar topics.

Whichever book is right for your reader, Blastoff! Readers are the perfect books to build confidence and encourage a love of reading that will last a lifetime!

This edition first published in 2014 by Bellwether Media, Inc.

No part of this publication may be reproduced in whole or in part without written permission of the publisher. For information regarding permission, write to Bellwether Media, Inc., Attention: Permissions Department, 5357 Penn Avenue South, Minneapolis, MN 55419.

Library of Congress Cataloging-in-Publication Data

Owings, Lisa.
Louisiana / by Lisa Owings.
    pages cm. – (Blastoff! readers. Exploring the states)
Includes bibliographical references and index.
Summary: "Developed by literacy experts for students in grades three through seven, this book introduces young readers to the geography and culture of Louisiana"–Provided by publisher.
ISBN 978-1-62617-017-9 (hardcover : alk. paper)
1. Louisiana–Juvenile literature. I. Title.
F369.3.O95 2013
976.3–dc23

2013006021

Table of Contents

Where Is Louisiana?	4
History	6
The Land	8
The Atchafalaya Basin	10
Wildlife	12
Landmarks	14
New Orleans	16
Working	18
Playing	20
Food	22
Festivals	24
Jazz	26
Fast Facts	28
Glossary	30
To Learn More	31
Index	32

Where Is Louisiana?

Louisiana lies in the southern United States at the **mouth** of the Mississippi River. The sole of this boot-shaped state rests on the **Gulf** of Mexico. Several islands are scattered off the southern coast.

Arkansas is Louisiana's neighbor to the north. The Sabine River forms part of the border with Texas to the west. To the east, the Mississippi River separates Louisiana from Mississippi. The capital of Louisiana is Baton Rouge. It stands on the banks of the Mississippi River in the southeastern part of the state.

Shreveport

Sabine River

Texas

Arkansas

Louisiana

Mississippi River

Mississippi

Atchafalaya Basin

Atchafalaya River

★ Baton Rouge

Lafayette

Metairie

New Orleans

N
W   E
S

Gulf of Mexico

History

Early peoples arrived in Louisiana more than
10,000 years ago. They hunted along the
Mississippi River and Gulf Coast. In 1541,
Spanish explorer Hernando de Soto came in
search of gold. The French followed in 1682. They
claimed the area and later settled there. In 1803,
France sold Louisiana to the United States in the
Louisiana Purchase. Louisiana became a state
in 1812.

Hernando
de Soto

Louisiana Timeline!

1541:	Hernando de Soto explores Louisiana. He searches for gold but finds none.
1682:	René-Robert Cavelier claims the land for France.
1760s:	The British force French-speaking Acadians out of Canada. The Acadians, or Cajuns, settle in southern Louisiana.
1803:	France sells land including most of Louisiana to the United States in the Louisiana Purchase.
1812:	Louisiana becomes the eighteenth state.
1861–1865:	Louisiana and other Southern states fight for independence from the United States in the Civil War.
1901:	Oil is discovered in southern Louisiana.
2005:	Hurricane Katrina strikes Louisiana's Gulf Coast. The storm floods New Orleans and kills more than 1,500 Louisianans.
2010:	An oil spill off Louisiana's coast fills the Gulf of Mexico with millions of gallons of oil. It takes three months to stop the spill. Coastal wildlife and businesses struggle to recover.

René-Robert Cavelier

Hurricane Katrina

oil spill

The Land

Lake Pontchartrain Causeway

fun fact

Lake Pontchartrain is Louisiana's largest lake. Running almost 24 miles (38 kilometers) across it is the Lake Pontchartrain Causeway. It is the world's longest bridge over water.

Louisiana is a flat state full of rivers, lakes, and wetlands. The Mississippi River shaped much of Louisiana. Over thousands of years, **silt** carried by the river built up. It formed the Mississippi **Delta**. The Delta extends far into the Gulf of Mexico.

Plains stretch out on both sides of the Mississippi. They are crisscrossed with rivers and **bayous**. Sand beaches and **marshes** line the coast. To the north and west, the wetlands give way to prairies and forested hills. Winters in Louisiana are mild. Summers are hot and damp. Louisianans prepare for **hurricanes** in summer and fall.

The Atchafalaya Basin

West of the Mississippi in southern Louisiana lies the Atchafalaya River. Its **basin** holds one of the nation's largest swamps. This wetland wilderness area is known for its bald cypress trees. Their trunks narrow as they rise over the swamp. Spanish moss hangs from their branches.

The Atchafalaya Basin is home to many wetland animals. Alligators break the surface of the still water. The calls of herons and hundreds of other birds fill the air. Human activities and natural disasters threaten life in this special place. Louisianans are working hard to protect the basin and its wildlife.

heron

Wildlife thrives in Louisiana's wetlands and forests. Alligators rule the southern swamps and marshes. These areas are also home to snowy egrets, great blue herons, and other birds. The **endangered** brown pelican nests along the coast. Tiny shrimps share Gulf waters with giant tarpons and rays.

wild hog

catfish

brown pelican

Did you know?
The American alligator can grow 15 feet (5 meters) long and weigh up to 1,000 pounds (450 kilograms). It has one of the most powerful bites on Earth!

Rivers and lakes hold bass and catfish. The Louisiana black bear roams along riverbanks. Woodlands shelter white-tailed deer, gray foxes, and wild hogs. Copperhead snakes slither across the forest floor underneath pine, oak, and magnolia trees. The magnolia's sweet-smelling blooms open in summer.

Landmarks

Saint Louis Cathedral

Louisiana's rich history makes it a popular vacation spot. Visitors to New Orleans stroll through the French Quarter. Charming old buildings line the streets. Their fine **ironwork** looks like lace. Jackson Square bustles beneath the **spires** of the Saint Louis Cathedral. The River Road stretches along the Mississippi between New Orleans and Baton Rouge. It is known for its classic southern **plantation** houses.

People head to southern Louisiana for a taste of Cajun food and music. Lush gardens, a bird **sanctuary**, and the Tabasco Pepper Sauce Factory await visitors to Avery Island. In Shreveport, more than 20,000 rosebushes bloom in the American Rose Center gardens.

Oak Alley Plantation

fun fact

The Oak Alley Plantation is one of the most photographed plantations in the state. It is named for the beautiful old oaks that line the walk to the plantation house.

New Orleans

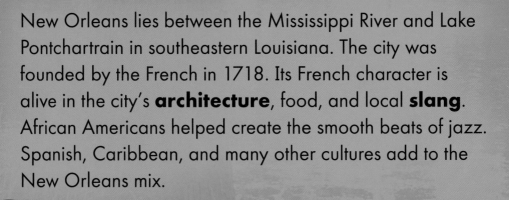

fun fact

New Orleans is said to be one of the most haunted cities in the country. Many visitors enjoy searching for ghosts in haunted places.

New Orleans lies between the Mississippi River and Lake Pontchartrain in southeastern Louisiana. The city was founded by the French in 1718. Its French character is alive in the city's **architecture**, food, and local **slang**. African Americans helped create the smooth beats of jazz. Spanish, Caribbean, and many other cultures add to the New Orleans mix.

French Quarter

Saint Charles Streetcar

New Orleans is still recovering from Hurricane Katrina. The city showed how far it has come when it hosted the 2013 Super Bowl. **Tourists** walk the streets of the French Quarter again. Travelers fill the seats of the Saint Charles Streetcar. Louisianans welcome them with music, dancing, and some of the best parties around.

Louisiana is rich in **natural resources**. Its soils support crops of sugarcane, cotton, and rice. Louisiana forests and tree farms provide much of the country's wood. Workers drill for oil and natural gas near Shreveport and off the Gulf Coast. In coastal waters, fishers fill their nets with shrimps, crabs, and oysters.

Factory workers turn the state's oil and natural gas into fuels and chemicals. They also produce wood, paper, and food products. Most Louisianans have **service jobs**. Government workers are centered in Baton Rouge. Workers in hotels, shops, and restaurants welcome the millions of tourists that visit the state each year.

Where People Work in Louisiana

manufacturing
6%

farming and
natural resources
5%

government
15%

services
74%

Playing

There is always something to do in Louisiana. Hunters and bird-watchers head for the woodlands and wetlands. Fishing is good in the rivers and coastal waters. Hikers and campers are drawn to the many state parks. Families wander through public gardens or picnic along the shores of Lake Pontchartrain. They head to the cities to enjoy concerts, plays, and art museums.

New Orleans is all about football. The city is home to the NFL's New Orleans Saints. It also hosts college football's Sugar Bowl each year. Basketball is another popular sport in the state.

fun fact !

New Orleans has hosted the Super Bowl ten times. That is more than any other city but Miami.

New Orleans
Saints

Food

gumbo

beignets

Louisiana is famous for its **Creole** and Cajun foods. Steaming bowls of gumbo are served throughout the state. This thick soup often features seafood, sausage, and a vegetable called okra. Many popular dishes use rice. *Étouffée* is a seafood stew served over rice. Jambalaya combines rice with a variety of meats, vegetables, and spices.

Sandwiches are a favorite New Orleans street food. Muffulettas are piled high with cold meats, cheeses, and olives. The classic po' boy is served on French bread. In spring, Louisianans gather to feast on boiled crawfish and corn on the cob. Sweet treats include pecan pie and French donuts called *beignets*.

Shrimp Po' Boy Sandwiches

Ingredients:

1 pound shrimp, peeled and devined

1 tablespoon Creole seasoning

1 cup cornmeal

1 1/2 cups flour

1 cup buttermilk

2 8-inch French rolls

Remoulade sauce

1 cup shredded lettuce

1 tomato, sliced

Vegetable oil for frying

Directions:

1. Heat oil in pan.

2. Pour buttermilk in a small bowl.

3. Mix flour, cornmeal, and Creole seasoning in a small bowl.

4. Dip shrimp in buttermilk, then in flour mixture. Fry coated shrimp in oil until golden brown.

5. Cut rolls horizontally, then coat cut sides in remoulade.

6. Layer lettuce, shrimp, and tomato on bread.

7. Serve with hot sauce. Makes 2 sandwiches.

Festivals

Mardi Gras parade

The biggest party in Louisiana is *Mardi Gras*. The *Mardi Gras* season lasts from January 6 until the beginning of **Lent** in February or March. People from all over the world crowd into New Orleans dressed in purple, green, and gold. There are weeks of dazzling parades. Beads, coins, and coconuts are thrown into the crowd from colorful floats. The celebrations get bigger as Lent draws closer.

king cake

Breaux Bridge hosts the Crawfish Festival each May. Louisianans gather to enjoy crawfish dishes, live music, and dancing. The festival's crawfish race is fun for all ages. The New Orleans Jazz and Heritage Festival spans a full week. It attracts big-name performers and more than 400,000 fans.

Jazz

Jazz is a soulful style of music that had its beginnings in New Orleans. African Americans introduced its swinging rhythms and bopping melodies in the early 1900s. Louis Armstrong and other New Orleans musicians often played what they felt instead of reading music. Jazz became a way of life in Louisiana. It has since influenced music all over the world.

The New Orleans Jazz National Historical Park celebrates the state's jazz heritage. Visitors can learn about jazz history, take walking tours, and attend regular concerts. Every evening, people fill jazz clubs across the state. Some sit back and listen. Others dance all night. The music is a perfect soundtrack to life in fun-loving, easygoing Louisiana.

fun fact

New Orleans native Louis Armstrong was one of the most famous jazz musicians of all time. He was known for his trumpet skills and deep, gritty voice.

Louis Armstrong

27

Fast Facts About Louisiana

Louisiana's Flag

Louisiana's flag has a blue background. In the center is a mother pelican caring for her young. The pelican represents sacrifice and protection. A banner below the pelican displays the state's motto.

State Flower

magnolia

State Nicknames:	The Pelican State The Bayou State The Sugar State
State Motto:	"Union, Justice, and Confidence"
Year of Statehood:	1812
Capital City:	Baton Rouge
Other Major Cities:	New Orleans, Shreveport, Metairie, Lafayette
Population:	4,533,372 (2010)
Area:	47,632 square miles (123,366 square kilometers); Louisiana is the 31st largest state.
Major Industries:	mining, forestry, farming, services, manufacturing
Natural Resources:	oil, natural gas, salt, sulfur, clay
State Government:	105 representatives; 39 senators
Federal Government:	6 representatives; 2 senators
Electoral Votes:	8

State Animal
Louisiana black bear

State Bird
brown pelican

Glossary

architecture—the style of buildings

basin—an area of land surrounding a river; the water from a basin drains into a river.

bayous—small, slow-moving streams that connect to other bodies of water

Creole—people related to early French and Spanish settlers in Louisiana

delta—the area around the mouth of a river

endangered—at risk of becoming extinct

gulf—part of an ocean or sea that extends into land

hurricanes—spinning rainstorms that start over warm ocean waters

ironwork—something made of iron, such as decorative structures on buildings

Lent—the forty weekdays before the Christian holiday of Easter; *Mardi Gras* is a final celebration before the Lenten season of giving up certain foods and activities.

Louisiana Purchase—a deal made between France and the United States; the Louisiana Purchase gave the United States 828,000 square miles (2,144,510 square kilometers) of land west of the Mississippi River.

marshes—wetlands with grasses and plants

mouth—a place where a river empties into a larger body of water

natural resources—materials in the earth that are taken out and used to make products or fuel

plains—large areas of flat land

plantation—a large farm that grows coffee, cotton, rubber, or other crops; plantations are mainly found in warm climates.

sanctuary—a place of safety and protection

service jobs—jobs that perform tasks for people or businesses

silt—a fine, dirt-like material that comes from rocks; silt is carried and deposited by rivers.

slang—words used in casual conversation

spires—towers that come to a point on top of buildings

tourists—people who travel to visit another place

To Learn More

AT THE LIBRARY

Benoit, Peter. *The Louisiana Purchase*. New York, N.Y.: Children's Press, 2012.

San Souci, Robert D. *Little Pierre: A Cajun Story from Louisiana*. San Diego, Calif.: Harcourt, Inc., 2003.

Tarshis, Lauren. *I Survived Hurricane Katrina, 2005*. New York, N.Y.: Scholastic, 2011.

ON THE WEB

Learning more about Louisiana is as easy as 1, 2, 3.

1. Go to www.factsurfer.com.

2. Enter "Louisiana" into the search box.

3. Click the "Surf" button and you will see a list of related Web sites.

With factsurfer.com, finding more information is just a click away.

Index

activities, 15, 16, 17, 20, 24, 25, 26
American Rose Center, 15
Armstrong, Louis, 26
Atchafalaya Basin, 5, 10-11
Baton Rouge, 4, 5, 15, 19
capital (see Baton Rouge)
climate, 9
Crawfish Festival, 25
festivals, 24-25
food, 15, 16, 22-23, 25
French Quarter, 15, 17
history, 6-7, 15, 16, 17, 26
Hurricane Katrina, 7, 17
Jackson Square, 15
Jazz, 16, 25, 26-27
Lake Pontchartrain, 8, 16, 20
landmarks, 14-15
landscape, 8-11
location, 4-5
Mardi Gras, 24, 25
Mississippi River, 4, 5, 6, 8, 9, 10, 15, 16
New Orleans, 5, 7, 15, 16-17, 20, 22, 24, 25, 26
New Orleans Jazz and Heritage Festival, 25
New Orleans Jazz National Historical Park, 26
Oak Alley Plantation, 15
River Road, 15
Saint Charles Streetcar, 17
Saint Louis Cathedral, 14, 15
sports, 17, 20
Sugar Bowl, 20
Super Bowl, 17, 20
Tabasco Pepper Sauce Factory, 15
wildlife, 7, 10, 12-13
working, 18-19

The images in this book are reproduced through the courtesy of: Gary718, front cover (bottom), pp. 14-15; (Collection)/ Prints & Photographs Division/ Library of Congress, pp. 6, 7 (left); National Oceanic & Atmospheric Administration, p. 7 (middle); U.S. Coast Guard/ Zuma Press/ Newscom, p. 7 (right); David Frazier/ Corbis/ Glow Images, p. 8 (small); Exactostock/ SuperStock, pp. 8-9; Mlorenz, p. 10; Corbis/ SuperStock, pp. 10-11; Clara, pp. 12-13; Eduard Kyslynskyy, p. 13 (top); Gpflman, p. 13 (middle); A9photo, p. 13 (bottom); Zack Frank, p. 15 (small); Pixelchrome – Jeremy Woodhouse/ SuperStock, pp. 16-17; Ron Buskirk/ Age Fotostock/ SuperStock, p. 17 (top); Ray Laskowitz/ SuperStock, p. 17 (bottom); Michael Ventura/ Alamy, p. 18; AP Photo/ Eric Gay/ Associated Press, p. 19; Action Sports Photography, p. 20 (small); Jeff Greenberg/ Age Fotostock, pp. 20-21; Jabiru, p. 22 (top); Jose Gil, p. 22 (bottom); Kcline, p. 23; Dlewis33, pp. 24-25; Cheryl Casey, p. 25 (small); Marka/ SuperStock, p. 26; Visions of America/ SuperStock, pp. 26-27; Pakmor, p. 28 (top); Le Do, p. 28 (bottom); Cliff Collings, p. 29 (left); Denis Pepin, p. 29 (right).